Table of Contents

Meet BWA's Lead Editor and Author Ms. Valerie Staton. as she adds a new book to her library!

Ariel Cooper

Literary Moments

Everything Authors need to know about writing their manuscript to publishing their work, as well as educational information, inspiration, and tools of the industry.

Valerie Staton

Paulette Henson

BWA Magazine Editor in Chief: A Message to Our Readers
Celebrating our Sisters Through Words

In the world of literature, Black women authors have shared stories filled with resilience, wisdom, and beauty, creating narratives that highlight their unique experiences. BWA Magazine proudly celebrates these voices, which continue to impact readers across generations and cultures.

Empowering Narratives

Our authors explore themes like identity, heritage, and empowerment, offering inspiration and hope through powerful memoirs and captivating fiction. Each issue of BWA Magazine showcases their brilliance and storytelling expertise.

Unveiling Untold Stories

BWA Magazine brings hidden histories to light and amplifies the voices of Black women authors, who confront injustices and reclaim their narratives. Their stories guide us toward a more inclusive and equitable world.

Platform for Expression

BWA Magazine is a platform where Black women authors celebrate their achievements and connect with a diverse audience. Through interviews, essays, and book features, we honor their contributions to literature.

Inspiring Future Generations

Black women authors are shaping future generations, sparking change, and promoting equality. BWA Magazine is dedicated to supporting and elevating these voices to ensure their legacies continue.

Join the Celebration

Each issue of BWA Magazine is a celebration of Black womanhood and a tribute to the powerful voices in literature. Explore these transformative stories and be part of the legacy.

Paulette Henson

How to Write a Mystery Book: Crafting Suspense and Intrigue
By Paulette Henson

Writing a mystery book is a unique challenge that requires a blend of creativity, logical thinking, and attention to detail. Whether you're crafting a cozy whodunit or a gritty crime thriller, the key to a successful mystery lies in engaging readers with a compelling puzzle while keeping them guessing until the very end. Here's a step-by-step guide to help you write a gripping mystery novel.

1. Choose Your Subgenre

Before you begin writing, decide on the type of mystery you want to create. Mystery novels come in various subgenres, each with its own tone and style:

- **Cozy Mysteries:** Lighthearted and often set in small towns with amateur sleuths. Think Agatha Christie's Miss Marple or Jessica Fletcher in Murder, She Wrote.

- **Crime Thrillers:** Darker and grittier, these often involve law enforcement or private investigators solving violent crimes. Examples include The Girl with the Dragon Tattoo by Stieg Larsson.

- **Police Procedurals:** Focuses on the police force's step-by-step investigation, emphasizing realism and procedural accuracy. Think Michael Connelly's Harry Bosch series.

Knowing your subgenre helps you establish tone, plot direction, and character types.

2. Start with a Strong Hook

A mystery novel should immediately grab the reader's attention. Begin with a scene that presents a problem or mystery that will carry the story forward. The hook can be the discovery of a body, an unexplained disappearance, or a crime witnessed by someone unreliable. This initial intrigue pulls readers in and sets the stage for the mystery.

3. Develop an Intriguing Detective or Sleuth

Your main character, whether a professional detective, amateur sleuth, or accidental investigator, needs to be someone readers want to follow. Consider:

- Background: What skills, knowledge, or life experiences make them suited to solving this mystery? Do they have any unique quirks or methods of investigation?
- Motivation: Why do they care about solving this case? Personal stakes or moral obligations make the detective more engaging.
- Flaws: Give your sleuth some flaws or vulnerabilities. A character who struggles with something internal, whether it's self-doubt or a troubled past, adds depth to the story.

4. Craft a Compelling Crime or Puzzle

At the heart of every mystery is the crime that must be solved. This could be a murder, theft, disappearance, or other intrigue. To create a compelling crime:

- Be Original: Avoid overused tropes. Try to give your crime a unique twist that hasn't been done before.
- Provide Multiple Layers: A mystery is more gripping when there are multiple suspects, each with their own secrets or motives. Subplots and red herrings (false clues) can keep readers guessing.
- Plan the Solution First: Know who committed the crime and why before you start writing. This allows you to plant clues and misdirects carefully throughout the book.
- 5. Set the Scene with a Vivid Setting
- Your setting plays a significant role in creating the atmosphere and mood of your mystery. Whether it's a foggy small town, a bustling city, or a remote mansion, the setting should contribute to the story's tone.
- Use Sensory Detail: Describe the smells, sounds, and sights of the location to immerse readers.
- Incorporate Setting into the Plot: The location can serve as a character itself. For example, a small town may harbor deep secrets, while a big city might be a maze of anonymity.

6. Introduce Compelling Suspects

Your mystery needs a cast of suspects, each with potential motives and secrets. Well-developed suspects are essential to keeping readers on their toes. Consider:

- Motives: Why might each character want to commit the crime? Jealousy, revenge, financial gain, or hidden pasts are classic motives.
- Red Herrings: Create false leads to misdirect both the detective and the reader. These false clues can add tension and complexity to the story.
- Distinct Personalities: Each suspect should have a distinct voice, background, and relationship to the victim or crime.

7. Plant Clues and Red Herrings Carefully

The clues and evidence you present should be sprinkled throughout the story. Avoid giving away too much too early, but make sure the clues are fair—readers should have a chance to figure it out.

- Clues: These can be physical objects, pieces of dialogue, or inconsistencies in characters' alibis. They should point to the real culprit, even if subtly.
- Red Herrings: False clues should appear convincing at first but fall apart as more information is revealed. These help maintain suspense and intrigue.

8. Build Tension with Pacing

Mystery novels thrive on suspense, and you can create that by pacing the revelation of information and raising the stakes as the story progresses.

- Slow Reveals: Don't give too much information too soon. Let the sleuth uncover clues gradually, piecing things together while encountering setbacks.
- Raise the Stakes: As the detective gets closer to solving the mystery, introduce new dangers or obstacles. Maybe the culprit becomes aware they're being hunted and tries to silence the detective or another person is targeted.

9. Write an Explosive Climax and Satisfying Resolution

The climax is the moment where the mystery is solved and the culprit revealed. This should be an exciting and rewarding moment for both the characters and the readers.

- The Reveal: Ideally, the reveal should be surprising but logical. Readers should be able to look back and recognize the clues that pointed to the solution.

PAULETTE HENSON"
hello@reallygreatsite.com

- Resolution: Tie up loose ends and explain how the detective arrived at their conclusion. Readers want to feel satisfied that all the threads of the mystery have been resolved.

10. Edit and Refine

Once your first draft is complete, take time to refine your manuscript. Pay attention to:

- Consistency: Ensure that all clues and character actions align with the solution. Check for any plot holes or inconsistencies.

- Pacing: Does the story flow smoothly? Are there moments where the tension lags? Trim any unnecessary scenes to keep the story focused.

- Character Depth: Make sure your sleuth and suspects are fully fleshed out and compelling.

Conclusion

Writing a mystery book requires balancing suspense, character development, and intricate plotting. By following these steps—crafting a compelling crime, developing complex characters, planting clues and red herrings, and building toward an exciting resolution—you can write a mystery that captivates readers and keeps them guessing until the final page. Happy writing!

AUTHOR
Davina Ward

Davina Ward is an Author and Certified Christian Life Coach commissioned by God to free women and help them understand that resilience is possible - no matter what they have endured. She has experienced a vast array of challenges that have authenticated and motivated her to share her experiences with other vulnerable women.

She commonly refers to herself as the P.U.S.H. Coach, (Persist, Until, Satan, Halts), due to her effective coaching approach that guides women into learning how to discover and tap into their purpose through the tearing down of their limiting beliefs and insecurities.

Her program and teachings provide strategies to remove layers of lies, doubt, and shame that paralyze women of purpose.

Davina partners with her clients as they shift their focus from the reflection they see in the mirror to the warrior God designed them to be in the spirit. Her main goal is personal development leaving her clients feeling equipped and worthy to walk into what God has purposed them to do and be.

Her true passion lies in walking beside vulnerable women to awaken their inner selves as they enter into their destiny.

In addition to her life's work, Davina has an extensive background in the public sector working with individuals with modest means. She was born and raised in New Jersey and resides with her husband, Reverend Robert Ward. She delights in being a mother to 3 sons and a grandmother to 2 grandchildren. She delights in serving in her local church and community.

MISS-ADVENTURES LOVE COACHING
EMPOWERING WOMEN ON ALL ASPECTS OF LOVE

Stephanie is a Certified Master Life Coach, the CEO of Miss-Adventures, LLC, three-time #1 Bestselling author, and #1 New Release. Stephanie's mission is empowering women on all aspects of love. She strongly believes in the power of prayer and affirmations to ignite and create the love, health, wealth, success, family, abundance, relationships, and prosperity we want in our lives. Stephanie is a podcaster, public speaker, published writer—over 250 articles between hubpages, Paired Life and Elephant Journal. She has also been a guest on multiple radio and podcast shows. Stephanie has been mentoring women for over 26-plus years and offers in-person and virtual sessions.

STEPHANIE BAILEY

BENEFITS OF SELF-LOVE:

- Personal Growth
- Using your voice—not being afraid to speak up.
- Confronting your fears.
- Empowering yourself through forgiveness—to release being a victim.
- And more…

"Stephanie is an exceptionally valuable expert on relationship advice. Over the years her wisdom and guidance have been at the core of my personal growth on my journey. xoxoxo Love you!"

— NANCY G., COLORADO

CONTACT:

323-332-9976
MISS-ADVENTURES.COM

MISS-ADVENTURES.COM

RETURN OF THE EX–LIVING DEAD!

BY

STEPHANIE BAILEY

Return of the Ex- Living Dead

Have you ever gone to a restaurant, bar, grocery store, etc., and bumped into someone that you used to date casually or for an extended period, but since things ended with this person, maybe unbeknownst to you (Disappearing Act/Ghosted—types of men from my book 99 Types of Guys: A Humorous Collection of Dating Tips and Misadventures), and you haven't seen or spoken to them? This type of situation I call the Return of the Ex-Living Dead—similar to the Living Dead —the movie with zombies, except he's clearly alive.

Since your ex-living dead lacked immaturity and didn't officially end the relationship but instead Ghosted you—he thought he would never see or speak to you again. Ouch. This unexpected reunion is not pleasant.

The Return of the Ex-Living Dead mimics the characteristics of a zombie:

• He hasn't called, texted, emailed, or Snapchat.

• He is no longer in your life.

• He acts like he doesn't know or remember you when he sees you.

• He has difficulty forming words or complete sentences when you speak.

• Doesn't look into your eyes.

• He fidgets a lot.

• In your mind, he's "dead to you" since he disappeared without a trace.

When you see the Return of the Ex-Living Dead, there is an awkward, uncomfortable feeling between you two—like being chased by Jason from Halloween, but there's nowhere to run and hide. You're uncomfortable and need to escape with poise, sophistication, and unobvious lightning speed.

This unamusing, immature disappearing act is incredibly frustrating because you didn't see any signs indicating his quick and sudden departure from your life. It's also a massive blow to the self-ego (why me?).

To keep life exciting, there is usually a time when the Return Of the Ex-Living Dead rises back into your life—similar to a zombie movie—but hopefully without the screams of terror and pains of being eaten alive.

Return Of The Ex... (Cont))

Seeing Multiple Men You've Dated In One Night Can Be An Overkill.
The Return of the Ex-Living Dead multiplied for me since I ended up at various venues in one night. Talk about a horror movie. Luckily, I was surrounded by my beautiful female posse(always helpful in these situations). I looked stunning with my high-heeled boots, fitted jeans, sexy off-the-shoulder top, and an exceptionally excellent hair day.
The ex-living dead seemed to follow me everywhere I went, and a new one would suddenly appear. This felt like my own zombie movie and worst nightmare at the same time. Lucky for me, my friends found humor in the situation, which, of course, lightened the mood that could have been horrific.
Remain Cool, Smile and Leave With Grace.
If you ever run into your ex-living dead, remember: remain cool—never let them see you freak out—smile, and continue to have fun. Exit the venue as soon as possible with grace; avoid running for the door (you don't want to draw attention). If you happen to make eye contact, smile and nod hello, and for the sake of conversation, keep it composed, short, and sweet (avoid drama at all costs).
Here's the thing, having anyone vanish from your life without closure—especially if you were intimate—sucks. Unfortunately, we can't always know why a relationship ended. In my case, I felt seeing the ex-living dead (several of them) was a reminder of how lucky I feel to no longer have these men in my life. If a man doesn't have the decency to send a "goodbye, so long" text, why would you want them in your life? This type of behavior is a blessing in disguise.
Ladies, if you ever encounter the Return of the Ex-Living Dead, don't let him ruin your night. Remember, you can outrun most zombies (aka your ex), and there is always a reason why things happen the way they do. Be brave, hold your head high, and live your best life—without him.

Victoria Quinn
Author/Pastor
FACE OF DECEPTION
VICTORIA QUINN

SHENITA L YELL
CO-AUTHOR
THE TARNISHED CROWN

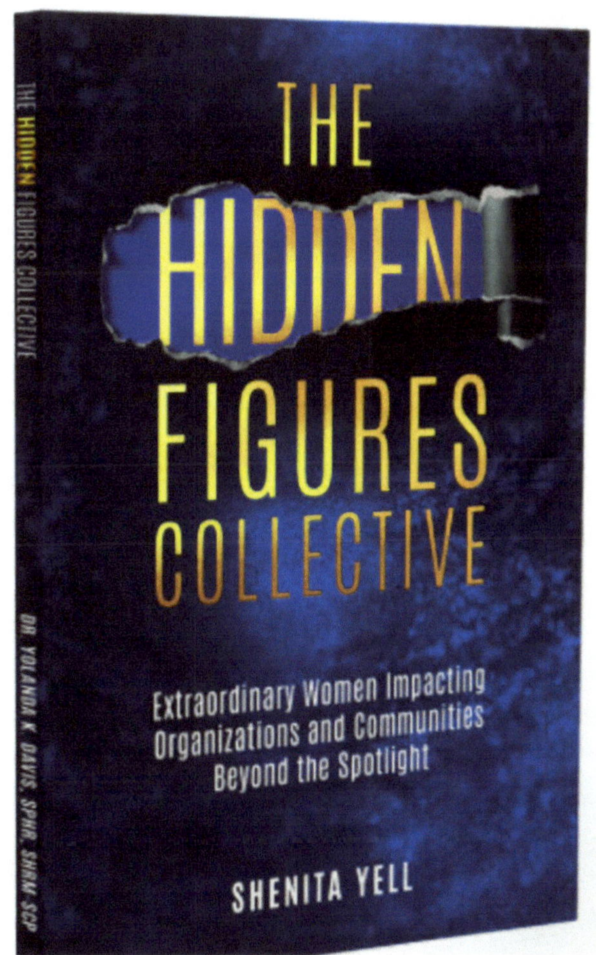

ARIEL COOPER

AUTHOR
BUSINESS WOMAN

FEATURED AUTHOR

Ariel Cooper

Ariel's Mission to Empower Women

Today, Ariel is on a mission to reach women facing similar challenges. She understands the unique struggles that many women endure, from battling addiction to seeking validation and love in all the wrong places. Ariel's experiences have equipped her with the empathy and insight needed to connect with women who feel lost, alone, and misunderstood.

Ariel has begun to speak out more publicly about her journey, sharing her story through writing, speaking engagements, and community outreach. She has started a support group specifically for women who are struggling with addiction, trauma, and spiritual battles. Through this group, Ariel provides a safe space for women to share their experiences, find support, and embark on their own journeys of healing and self-discovery.

In addition to her support group, Ariel is working on a book that delves deeper into her experiences and the lessons she has learned. She hopes that by sharing her story in greater detail, she can reach even more women who need to hear that they are not alone and that there is hope for a better future.

Ariel's Journey: From Darkness to Spiritual Awakening

Ariel's mission is clear: to empower women to reclaim their lives, find their voices, and embrace their true selves. She believes that every woman has the potential to overcome her demons and live a life of purpose and fulfillment. Through her tireless efforts, Ariel is making a difference, one woman at a time, proving that even the darkest nights can lead to the most radiant dawns.

Her story is not just one of personal triumph but a call to action for all women to stand up, speak out, and support each other. Ariel's journey is far from over, and as she continues to grow and evolve, she remains committed to her mission of helping women find strength, clarity, and love in their own lives.

Ariel, a dynamic young woman, has been haunted by a recurring nightmare since childhood, where she sees the world ending and herself plummeting into hell. Each dream begins differently but inevitably ends with the ground collapsing into a fiery abyss that swallows her. From a young age, Ariel could see spirits that tormented her both awake and asleep, leading to a lifelong fear of the dark. Her attempts to share these visions were met with disbelief, forcing her to suffer in silence.

In this silence, Ariel struggled with severe alcohol and sex addiction, alongside numerous failed relationships. Her lifelong quest for love, driven by deep-seated issues of paternal abandonment, only led to repeated heartbreak. Despite these setbacks, Ariel never lost hope in finding true love. However, feeling utterly alone and broken, she often found herself crying out for help, even in her sleep, but her pleas went unheard. No knight in shining armor came to rescue her. Confused and desperate, she questioned why she could see spirits when others could not.

In her darkest moments, Ariel contemplated suicide but ultimately chose to seek life and answers. She turned to God, beginning a journey of spiritual warfare to find both love and her true purpose. This marked a new chapter in her life, one where she fought for clarity and strength in facing the unseen forces that plagued her.

Ariel Cooper, Miami native, mother of 3, and author. Inspired by personal experiences and spiritual encounters. Known for connecting with others effortlessly. Passionate about writing, helping, shopping, and creativity.

ISBN 979-8-89383-436-9

Spines

9 798893 834369

Black Women Authors
Professor Paulette Henson & Michelle Hardy

BWA - EMPOWER YOUR WORDS
WEBINAR

Writing Tips, Author Experiences , Q & A

Panelist Inquiries email:
education@blackwomenauthors.net

Michelle Hardy

JOIN ME & 13,000 WOMEN

I have been given an opportunity to help train over 13,000 members in the Black Women Authors group with Professor Paulette Henson, the founder of the group. I am so excited about it. Join and share your book with over 13,000 existing and aspiring authors.

EMPOWER YOUR WORDS! WEBINAR & INFO SESSION

Join us! on Wednesday!
October 9th @ 4pm (pst)

for discussion &. information on this course, why you need it and how to register!

Email:
education@blackwomenauthors.net

email: education@blackwomenauthors.net

WHAT'S COOKING?

Fall Menu Ideas

#1 BUTTERNUT SQUASH SOUP WITH SAGE AND GARLIC CROUTONS

A creamy, velvety soup perfect for cool autumn days.

- Ingredients: Butternut squash, onions, garlic, vegetable broth, cream, fresh sage, butter, olive oil, salt, and pepper.

- Instructions: Roast cubed butternut squash with olive oil, salt, and pepper. Sauté onions and garlic, then add the roasted squash and broth. Simmer, blend until smooth, and stir in cream. Garnish with crispy sage leaves and homemade garlic croutons.

RECIPE # 2
APPLE CIDER GLAZED PORK CHOPS WITH ROASTED ROOT VEGETABLES

A hearty, savory meal infused with sweet autumn apple cider flavors.

- Ingredients: Bone-in pork chops, apple cider, Dijon mustard, fresh thyme, sweet potatoes, carrots, parsnips, olive oil, and rosemary.

- Instructions: Sear the pork chops, then glaze with a reduction of apple cider and mustard. Roast the root vegetables with olive oil, rosemary, and thyme. Serve the pork chops on a bed of roasted veggies with extra glaze drizzled on top.

RECIPE #3 PUMPKIN RISOTTO WITH PARMESAN AND ROASTED PECANS

Pumpkin Risotto with Parmesan and

Toasted Pecans

A rich, comforting dish perfect for

fall evenings.

- Ingredients: Arborio rice,
  pumpkin puree, chicken or
  vegetable broth, shallots, white
  wine, Parmesan cheese, butter,
  toasted pecans, nutmeg, and
  thyme.

- Instructions: Sauté shallots in
  butter, add rice, and deglaze
  with white wine. Gradually add
  broth, stirring until creamy. Fold
  in pumpkin puree, Parmesan,
  and a pinch of nutmeg. Top
  with toasted pecans and fresh
  thyme for a satisfying crunch.

RECIPE #4 PUMPKIN SPICE CHEESECAKE BARS

PUMPKIN SPICE CHEESECAKE BARS

INGREDIENTS:

CRUST:

- 2 CUPS GRAHAM CRACKER CRUMBS
- 1/4 CUP GRANULATED SUGAR
- 1/2 CUP UNSALTED BUTTER, MELTED

CHEESECAKE LAYER:

- 16 OZ CREAM CHEESE, SOFTENED
- 1 CUP GRANULATED SUGAR
- 2 LARGE EGGS
- 1 TSP VANILLA EXTRACT
- 1 CUP CANNED PUMPKIN PUREE (NOT PUMPKIN PIE FILLING)
- 1 TSP PUMPKIN PIE SPICE (OR A MIX OF CINNAMON, NUTMEG, AND CLOVES)
- 1/4 TSP GROUND GINGER (OPTIONAL)
- 1/4 TSP SALT

TOPPING:

- WHIPPED CREAM (OPTIONAL)
- A SPRINKLE OF CINNAMON OR NUTMEG FOR GARNISH (OPTIONAL)

INSTRUCTIONS:

1. PREHEAT THE OVEN: PREHEAT YOUR OVEN TO 350°F (175°C). LINE A 9X13-INCH BAKING DISH WITH PARCHMENT PAPER, LEAVING AN OVERHANG FOR EASY REMOVAL LATER.
2. PREPARE THE CRUST:
   - IN A BOWL, MIX THE GRAHAM CRACKER CRUMBS, MELTED BUTTER, AND SUGAR UNTIL THE TEXTURE RESEMBLES WET SAND.
   - PRESS THE MIXTURE EVENLY INTO THE BOTTOM OF THE PREPARED BAKING DISH.
   - BAKE FOR ABOUT 8-10 MINUTES OR UNTIL SLIGHTLY GOLDEN. LET IT COOL WHILE YOU MAKE THE FILLING.
3. MAKE THE CHEESECAKE LAYER:
   - IN A LARGE BOWL, BEAT THE SOFTENED CREAM CHEESE AND SUGAR UNTIL SMOOTH AND CREAMY.
   - ADD EGGS ONE AT A TIME, BEATING WELL AFTER EACH ADDITION.
   - ADD VANILLA EXTRACT AND MIX IN THE PUMPKIN PUREE, PUMPKIN PIE SPICE, SALT, AND GROUND GINGER. BEAT UNTIL COMBINED AND SMOOTH.

RECIPE #4 PUMPKIN SPICE CHEESECAKE BARS

- ASSEMBLE AND BAKE:
  - POUR THE PUMPKIN CHEESECAKE MIXTURE OVER THE COOLED CRUST, SPREADING IT EVENLY WITH A SPATULA.
  - BAKE FOR 35-40 MINUTES OR UNTIL THE CENTER IS SET AND NO LONGER JIGGLES WHEN GENTLY SHAKEN.
- COOL AND CHILL:
  - LET THE BARS COOL TO ROOM TEMPERATURE, THEN REFRIGERATE FOR AT LEAST 3-4 HOURS OR OVERNIGHT TO SET COMPLETELY.
- SERVE:
  - ONCE CHILLED, REMOVE THE CHEESECAKE BARS USING THE PARCHMENT OVERHANG AND CUT THEM INTO SQUARES.
  - TOP WITH A DOLLOP OF WHIPPED CREAM AND A SPRINKLE OF CINNAMON OR NUTMEG FOR EXTRA FALL FLAVOR (OPTIONAL).

ENJOY THESE CREAMY, SPICED PUMPKIN CHEESECAKE BARS AS A DECADENT FALL DESSERT! 🍂🎃

About the Author

Thandisizwe Chimurenga is an award winning, Los Angeles-based freelance journalist and writer.

She is the author of *No Doubt: The Murder(s) of Oscar Grant* (2014); *Reparations ... Not Yet: A Case for Reparations and Why We Must Wait* (2015); *Some of Us Are Brave: Interviews and Conversations with Sistas on Life, Art and Struggle, Vols. 1 and 2* (2023/2024); and the co-author with Deborah Jones of *What We Stood For: The Story of a Revolutionary Black Woman* (2024).

Chimurenga is also a contributor to the following anthologies/edited collections: *2020: The Year That Changed America: Kevin Powell's Writing Workshop* (Bowker Books, 2021); the *Black Power Encyclopedia* (Greenwood Press, 2018); *Jackson Rising: The Struggle for Economic Democracy and Black Self-Determination in Jackson, Mississippi* (Daraja Press, 2017); *Why Don't The Poor Rise Up?* (AK Press, 2017); *Black Lives Matter: Lifespan Perspectives* (IndoAmerican Press, 2017); *Who Do You Serve, Who Do You Protect?* (Haymarket Books, 2016); *Killing Trayvons: An Anthology of American Violence* (CounterPunch Books, 2014); UCLA's *Amerasia* Journal in tribute to Japanese-American activist Yuri Kochiyama (Vol. 40, No. 3, 2014); and *Fertile Ground: Memories and Visions* (Runagate Press, 1996).

NO DOUBT
THE MURDER(S) OF
OSCAR GRANT
IF YOU WANT TO GET AWAY WITH MURDER BECOME A COP
THANDISIZWE CHIMURENGA

Valerie Staton

Valerie D. Staton is a writer/poet from New Jersey. Her latest book entitled "Journey to Wellness: A Personal Health Recordkeeper" is the perfect resource for keeping track of personal health information, such as: pharmacy/physician contact information, prescriptions, medication administration, allergies, vaccinations, medical tests (labs, surgeries, doctor visits, imaging). Daily tracking sheets have areas for tracking vitals, diet, medication administration, pain management, physical fitness activities and sleep. Journey to Wellness - is the perfect resource for patients and caregivers and the perfect gift, for those on your list.

"Staton the Facts" Informative Bible-Based Activity Book has over 1,200 activities! Inside its pages partakers will find words to unscramble, characters/locations to match, words to find, speakers to identify, bible verses to complete, and scriptural cryptograms to solve.

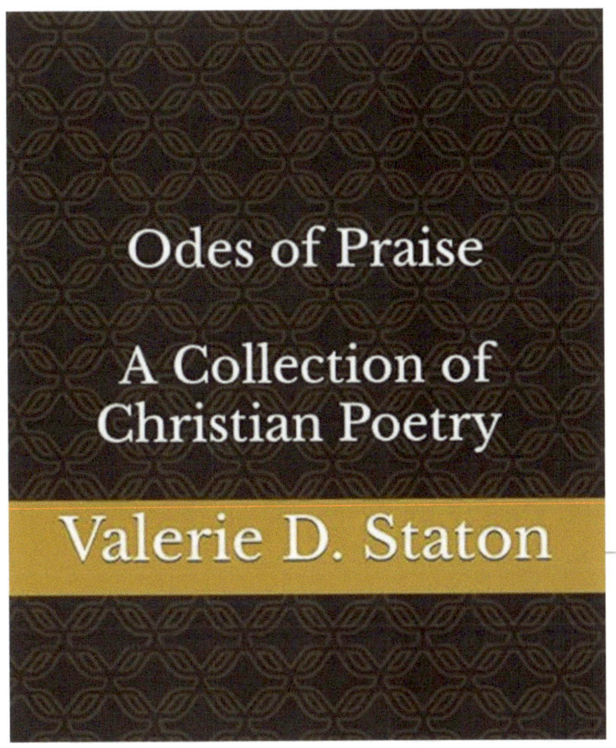

VALERIE STATON

Odes of Praise: A Collection of Christian Poetry" is a Christian based book of poetry, edifying our Lord and Savior Jesus Christ for the good work He has done and continues to do in our lives each day. Topics include, sin, crucifixion, love, mercy, grace, redemption, sanctification, salvation, fellowship, worship, deliverance, and praise.

Valerie has contributed poetry in Haiku, 50 Haikus, and Three Line Poetry journals published by Prolific Press and in the following poetic anthologies: PS: It's Poetry, Volume I, An Anthology of Eclectic Contemporary Poems Written by Poets from Around the Globe and PS: It's Still Poetry, Volume II, An Anthology of Eclectic Contemporary Poems Written by Poets from Around the Globe, published by Arczis Web Technologies, Inc. In her spare time the author likes to read, write, make jewelry and antique shop.

VALERIE STATON

Dr. Lisa L. Campbell

Dr. Lisa L. Campbell, known as "The Growth Motivator™," is the author of the inspirational book "Grow With Me." In this book, Dr. Lisa shares her journey of overcoming significant personal and professional challenges. Through vivid storytelling and heartfelt reflections, she shares her life lessons on resilience, faith, and personal growth. Her journey as an author began with a desire to inspire others, and she has developed a motivational writing style that connects deeply with readers. "Grow With Me" encourages readers to shed the weight of their burdens, embrace change, and pursue their dreams with determination and confidence. Dr. Lisa's engaging narrative and genuine voice make her book an uplifting and transformative read.

Doris Pinkett "Pinke Loved"

Presidential Lifetime Achievement Award Recipient, and Self-Published Author of "REFRESHED: A Journey of Reflections and Connections", Doris Pinkett is the founder of The Pinke Loved Institute, a platform designed to uplift women, particularly divorced women as they engage into new experiences and reset their lives after divorce. Doris jumped into the world of writing a few years after her 16-year marriage shockingly ended due to a $500 disagreement. The growth and revelations she experienced are penned inside this book. This Women's Empowerment Speaker has a sincere desire to uplift and celebrate women, as they make a comeback, and excel in every area of their lives. A native of Atlanta, Georgia, and a graduate of the Tennessee State University, Doris is the proud mother of 3 adult children, Nemiah (24), Melaiah (22) and JaH'son (21), all of whom are pursuing college degrees, and are leaders in their own right. Whether it be through her speaking, writing or her "REFRESHED" Yoga series, she aspires to engage, elevate, encourage, enlighten and empower women so they can maximize their purpose, both personally and professionally.

****

20/20 Enterprises Certified Speaker
Breathe for Change Certified Yoga and SEL Facilitator
2023 Sisterhood-On-The-Go Community Service Award Recipient

AVAILABLE ON AMAZON

<u>For Bookings and Inquiries</u>:
Phone Number: 404-207-7212
Website: https://linktr.ee/Pinkeloved
Facebook: Pinke Loved
Instagram: pinkelovedinstitute
Email: pinkelovedllc@gmail.com

A
WIDOW
AND A
FRIEND
STELLA STELLA

Literary
MOMENTS

A One-Stop Shop
For Authors

THE POET'S LOUNGE

open MIC

UPCOMING SHOWS
4PM (PST)
7PM (EST)

OCT. 4

NOV. 1

DEC. 6

PODCAST

LIVE ON
FACEBOOK/YOUTUBE

4PM (PST)

1st Friday of every month!

Attn: Poets
Speak on our Show!

Join Paulette

JOIN ZOOM MEETING
HTTPS://US06WEB.ZOOM.US/J/84367424989

MEETING ID: 843 6742 4989

Time Management *Strategies* for Authors

by Valerie Staton

PRIORITIZE TASKS

As an author, your time is precious. Priortize your tasks based on their importance and urgency. Use a to-do list or productivity app to organize your tasks and focus on completing the most crucial ones first. Delegate or outsource tasks that can be handled by others, freeing up your time for writing.

SCHEDULE WRITING TIME

Treat writing time as a non-negotiable appointment. Schedule specific hours in your day dedicated solely to writing. Stick to this schedule as much as possible, even when faced with distractions or other obligations. Having a designated writing time helps you build a consistent writing routine and stay on track.

MINIMIZE DISTRACTIONS

Create a distraction-free environment while you write. Turn off notifications, find a quiet space, or use noise-canceling headphones. If possible, write during times when you are less likely to be interrupted. By reducing distractions, you can focus more effectively on your writing and avoid wasting time on unnecessary interruptions.

BREAK DOWN LARGE PROJECTS

Overwhelming writing projects can lead to procrastination. Break time down into smaller, manageable chunks. Set realistic goals for each chunk and focus on completing one task at a time. This approach makes large projects seem less daunting and allows you to make steady progress.

UTILIZE TECHNOLOGY

Leverage technology to streamline your workflow. Use writing software that offers features such as auto-save, grammar checking, and distraction-free writing modes. Explore writing tools that help you track progress, manage research, and connect with other authors.

REGULARLY ASSESS ROUTINE

Lastly, good time management is not a one-size-fits-all approach. Regularly assess your routines and determine what's working and what isn't. Be open to change; your schedule should evolve as your needs change. Incorporate feedback from your productivity experiments, and don't hesitate to tweak your daily practices until you find the perfect balance for your writing life.

Effective time management is crucial for every author aspiring to bring their stories to life. By understanding your unique writing rhythm, setting clear goals, scheduling your writing, and embracing flexibility, you'll discover that you have the power to wield time in your favor. As you hone these skills, you'll find that writing moves from being a mere task to an engaging, joyous, and sustainable journey.

AUTHOR-PRENEURSHIP

My name is Michelle Hardy. I am excited for the opportunity to help educate and embrace so many women on a platform where the goal is the same: Publish books to impact people. I have been writing ever since I was 10 years old. I have a wide range of experience with the ups and down of writing and publishing books. My motto is "dropping books like albums." I hope to help you all do just that on this journey.

At BWA, our goal is to educate new and blossoming writer's on how to write and publish books.

I provide a constant resource of information through BWA Facebook posts, as well as my Youtube channel @SolitudeWithMichelle.

Whether you are just budding; wanting to finally complete a writing project, or already seasoned, I'm more than happy to help you on your journey from writing to publishing your book.

Online Classes - Coming Jan 25

BWA proudly announces it's first course to help our strong community build the best possible quality book for it's members and their target audience. Author-Preneurship 101 taught by Professor Paulette Henson and myself is an author business writing course designed to help new and seasoned authors get published in a one-stop shop. Being a new author can be challenging, but BWA is here to make things go as smooth as possible with a complete writing and publishing process. I invite you to sign up at the link below for our January 2025 course or send an email to education@blackwomenauthors.net for more information.

Click here to sign up

TIP OF THE MONTH

Many of us as authors, want to price our book based on looks. We'll say "I think my book should be $XYZ.99," because it looks good; however we need to remember your book is only going sell based on how well you market it, the quality information you provide and it's appropriate price in market place. The price point for your type of book is not based on how you are feeling that day. Take time to research the books in your genre and see what the price points are for print, digital (ebook) and audio so you can be competitive.

@SolitudeWithMichelle, or email me at Education@BlackWomenAuthors.net, and I'm more than happy to help you on your journey to publishing your book.

Got Questions? Hit me up!

Granny's Corner
By April W. aka Granny.

Who would have thought a small gesture, like laying in my bed on a Saturday morning with a good book (one of my favorite passions) would be so deeply rooted in my son's life. Today, both are 30-ish yrs young and avid readers. Often, they read more than me.
I was a single mother, and I worked full-time to make ends meet. With two growing boys there were no funds for extracurricular activities, so our Saturday morning ritual; my boys would lay in my bed and together, we read a book, followed by a trip to our local library. They loved hanging out in my bed at the end of each hectic week because it was also our bonding time.

This went on for years until I looked up and my growing boys were crowding me out of my bed. So, for my own comfort, I kicked them out and onto the floor. Their new positions on the floor didn't matter one bit. By then, they were both infatuated with knowledge.

At times when I didn't have a book ready for them, we just picked up a dictionary or encyclopedia. I would jokingly tease them that they have a brain full of useless information… My baby son says he still looks through thick informational books so he can talk with anyone about anything. They both brag that between a dictionary and an encyclopedia they can speak on a variety of subjects.
Today, they tell their children - my grandchildren, there is no need to ask daddy "why", because they too can read, they can look up answers on their own.

Granny's Corner
(Cont.)

I now have four granddaughters. I introduced them to the library as soon as they were walking. The world has evolved so much with computers and technology. We do some stuff on computers, but they have a genuine love and appreciation for books. We go to the local library regularly and each of them has their own library cards. Our librarians even know their names.

My granddaughters enjoy our library outings so much that I often lose track of the hours that speed by when we are there. It's one of the best venues for spending quality time. Gone are the days of reading through thick and heavy dictionaries and encyclopedias. It's bittersweet, because sometimes, I really miss the days when my son's would ask "why mommy why"!

Be sure to know and expose your children and grandchildren to the local library. It doesn't cost much and it tops the list of ways to spend quality time. Keep reading!

What I'm currently reading: Kept by Delphine Mitchell Brown

One of my favorite reads: Fed Up With The Fanny by Franklin White

A great recommendation: Finding Me by Viola Davis

Geek-Squad

Publishing & Tech Services

- Website Creation & Design
- Book/Video Trailers & Promotion
- Book Covers
- Formatting & Conversion
- SEO/Keyword Needs
- Social Media Management
- Website Maintenance
- Custom Help & Assistance

<u>**CLICK HERE**</u> to submit your needs; please allow 24 hrs for response.

it.services@BlackWomenAuthors.net

SAFEGUARDING CREATIVITY IN THE AGE OF AI

VICTORIA PEARSON

Safeguarding Creativity in the Age of AI: Strategies for Copyright Protection and Online Content Security in Book Publishing In today's digital age, where technology has revolutionized how we create, share, and consume content, the concept of copyright has never been more critical—especially in the realm of book publishing. As artificial intelligence (AI) and other advanced technologies continue to shape the literary landscape, it's vital for authors, publishers, and content creators to understand both the challenges and the opportunities that lie ahead. This article delves into the complexities of copyright protection in the digital era, focusing on AI's role in content creation, the challenges of online infringement, and strategies to secure intellectual property rights effectively.

The Evolving Landscape of Copyright in Book Publishing Copyright has traditionally served as a legal framework that grants exclusive rights to creators, protecting their original works from unauthorized use. However, the digital age has dramatically transformed this landscape, particularly in book publishing. The ease with which digital content can be replicated and distributed without permission has made copyright infringement a pervasive issue. For authors and publishers, protecting their works from piracy and unauthorized distribution is a growing concern.

The rapid advancements in AI have introduced new complexities to the copyright discussion. AI-generated content, for instance, raises questions about ownership and the extent to which copyright laws apply. As AI tools become more sophisticated, they can generate text that closely resembles human writing, blurring the lines between original and derivative works. For book publishers, this means navigating uncharted waters where traditional copyright principles may not fully apply.

SAFEGUARDING CREATIVITY IN THE AGE OF AI

Challenges of Copyright in the Digital Age

One of the primary challenges faced by copyright holders in the digital era is the sheer scale of content being produced and shared online. Every day, millions of new pieces of content are uploaded to the internet, making it nearly impossible to monitor and enforce copyright protections effectively. For authors and publishers, this can lead to rampant piracy, where unauthorized copies of books are shared freely across platforms, undermining both the financial and creative value of their work.

The anonymity of the internet further complicates the enforcement of copyright. Identifying and prosecuting infringers can be a daunting task, often leading to a game of cat and mouse where infringers find new ways to circumvent legal actions. This is particularly problematic in the book publishing industry, where the unauthorized distribution of digital books can happen across multiple platforms, from peer-to-peer sharing sites to social media.

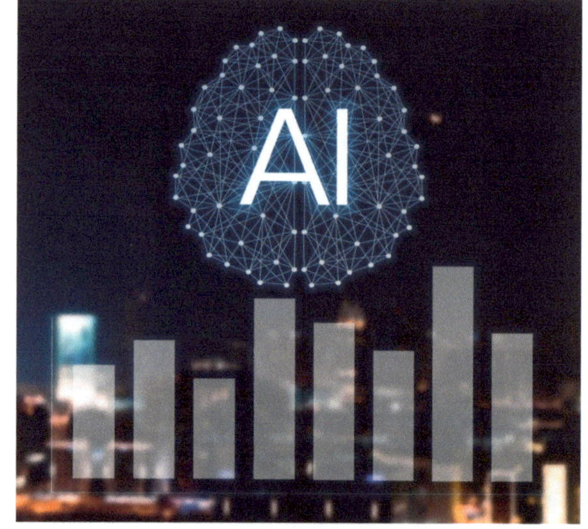

The Role of Digital Rights Management (DRM)

Digital Rights Management (DRM) has emerged as a key tool for protecting copyrighted content in the digital age. DRM technologies allow authors and publishers to control how their digital works are accessed, copied, and distributed. For example, DRM can restrict the number of times a digital book can be shared or limit access to only those who have purchased the content legally.

While DRM offers a level of protection, it is not without its drawbacks. Critics argue that DRM can be overly restrictive, sometimes penalizing legitimate users who may face difficulties in accessing their purchased content across different devices. Furthermore, determined infringers can often find ways to bypass DRM protections, rendering them less effective in some cases. Nevertheless, for book publishers, DRM remains an essential component of a broader strategy to protect intellectual property in the digital space.

Copyright and AI: Navigating New Challenges

The intersection of AI and copyright law presents new challenges for the publishing industry. AI-generated content raises fundamental questions about who owns the rights to these works. If an AI system creates a piece of text that is later published as a book, who holds the copyright—the developer of the AI, the user who inputted the data, or the AI itself?

Currently, copyright law does not fully account for works generated by non-human creators, leading to a legal gray area. This uncertainty can create potential conflicts over ownership and royalties, especially as AI tools become more integrated into the writing and publishing process. For authors, understanding the implications of using AI in their creative process is crucial to ensuring that their rights are protected.

Strategies for Protecting Content Online

In light of these challenges, authors and publishers must adopt comprehensive strategies to protect their works online. Here are several approaches that can help safeguard intellectual property in the digital age:

Watermarking and Metadata: Embedding digital watermarks and metadata into e-books can help track their distribution and identify unauthorized copies. This technology allows publishers to monitor where their content is being shared and take action if necessary.

Monitoring and Enforcement: Regularly monitoring the internet for unauthorized copies of your work is essential. Tools like web crawlers and content recognition software can help identify instances of infringement. Once identified, authors and publishers should be prepared to take swift action, whether through cease-and-desist letters or legal proceedings.

Legal Safeguards: Working with legal professionals to draft clear terms of use and licensing agreements can help protect your work. These documents should explicitly state how your content can be used and outline the consequences of unauthorized use.

Education and Awareness: Educating your audience about the importance of copyright and the consequences of infringement can foster a culture of respect for intellectual property. This can be done through blog posts, social media campaigns, and even within the content of your books.

Leveraging Technology: Beyond DRM, other technologies like blockchain are being explored as potential solutions for copyright protection. Blockchain can create an immutable record of ownership, making it easier to prove the originality and authorship of digital works.

Copyright Licensing and Monetization in Book Publishing

In addition to protecting content, authors and publishers should also consider how to effectively license and monetize their works in the digital age. Traditional publishing models may not be sufficient to address the challenges posed by digital distribution, but new opportunities are emerging.

Creative Commons Licensing: One approach is to use Creative Commons licenses, which allow creators to grant certain usage rights to the public while retaining copyright. This can help authors reach a wider audience while still maintaining control over their work.

Alternative Revenue Streams: Exploring alternative revenue streams such as crowdfunding, subscriptions, and direct sales through online platforms can provide additional income while reducing reliance on traditional publishing models. For example, platforms like Patreon allow authors to build a community of supporters who contribute financially in exchange for exclusive content.

Conclusion: Embracing the Future of Copyright in Publishing

As the digital landscape continues to evolve, the publishing industry must adapt to new challenges and opportunities. Protecting intellectual property in the age of AI requires a multifaceted approach that combines legal safeguards, technology, and education. By staying informed and proactive, authors and publishers can navigate the complexities of copyright in the digital era, ensuring that their creative works are protected and that they can continue to thrive in a rapidly changing environment.

The future of copyright in book publishing lies in embracing these new technologies and strategies, not just as a means of protection, but as tools for innovation and growth. By understanding the intricacies of copyright in the digital age, creators can safeguard their work while also exploring new ways to reach and engage with their audience.

As a BWA member, you have the opportunity to expand your knowledge and skills to assist in your journey as a self-published author through free courses on the grokly.me e-learning platform. Whether you want to safeguard your written works in the AI-driven publishing world, explore mindfulness, or learn the step-by-step process of becoming a self-published author, grokly.me offers valuable resources. Don't miss out on these limited-time opportunities—email Paulette directly or info@grokly.me to request the registration link to enroll in the Writer's Workshop today.

About the Author

Victoria Pearson, a professional with a diverse background spanning 26 years in technology, education, entrepreneurship, and community service, is a passionate advocate for community empowerment and education. She has served on the boards of various non-for-profit organizations and is a sought-after speaker and consultant. Pearson holds a bachelor's degree in psychology from UCLA and has completed concurrent master's-level studies in Health Administration and Gerontology. She is the founder of grokly.me, an innovative e-learning platform offering a diverse range of 550+ in-depth courses, ranging from The Writer's Workshop which includes 35+ courses for self-published authors, to artificial intelligence, business, wellness, personal growth, and reintegration for the formerly incarcerated. She is actively seeking partnerships with organizations and individuals who share her mission to democratize education and ignite passion for lifelong learning for disadvantaged persons. She can be reached at info@grokly.me.

The Author's Lounge
W/PAULETTE

Next Guest Author: You!

PROMOTE YOUR BOOK !

FOR MORE DETAILS

EMAIL:THEAUTHORSLOUNGETVSHOW@GMAIL.COM

WATCH ON FACEBOOK
(LIVE) BLACK WOMEN
AUTHORS
& YOUTUBE

LIKE/COMMENT/SHARE/SUBSCRIBE

BWA AUTHOR LEKECIA FORDHAM

Lekecia is a native of Charleston, S.C., and the founder of Lekecia Fordham Ministries LLC, which is an extension of her call to a life of worship and allows her to minister to God's people as an author, public speaker, minister of the gospel, blogger, and more. She is a Christian Author that has recently published her first book "Beautiful Lies vs. The Ugly Truth: Escaping Bondage and Embracing Freedom in Truth", which is currently available on Amazon, IngramSpark, and her website: www.lekeciafordhamministries.com.

This book was designed to be a tool that unveils the lies of the enemy that desires to keep us ensnared in the yokes of bondage. She undeniably understands the power of words and that faith comes by hearing and by hearing the word of God. In this vein, she is also the co-host of "Phone Nuggets Podcast" which is a Facebook and YouTube platform that encourages and edifies others in the wondrous Word of God.

BWA | *Author*
Lekecia Fordham

She is married to her love Richard and between them they have six wonderful children and five adorable grandchildren. Lekecia has always had a heart for others. As a child she desired to be a psychologist in hopes to help those hurting and suffering to cope with life. After giving her life to the Lord, that same desire and passion was revealed in the call to ministry. As a minister of the gospel, she ministers and comforts many in the faith by the grace of God. She finds her strength in the word of God and a life of prayer. She encourages others to know that with God all things are possible and that we can have a whole, complete, and full life in Him. Despite where you have been, if you allow Him, by faith God can make all things new. Her motto is ... "Your failures were never intended to be a muzzle, but a bullhorn!".

Social Media

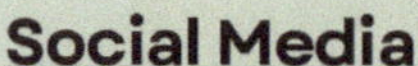

Instagram: Thelekeciafordham

Facebook: Lekecia Fordham

X (formerly Twitter): Lekeciafordham1

Amazon Book Link: https://amzn.to/4651PCv

Author
Erica N. Bryant

Erica N. Bryant is a wife and mother of two. She is an elementary educator and literacy advocate. Erica is the president and founder of Sparrow's Song Ministries (Sparrowssongministries.com), a group of believers who "just love Jesus." Her campaign: "The Word W.O.R.K.S." have helped women renew and strengthen their relationship with God by falling in love with His Word. Erica serves faithfully at her home church, Strait Gate Deliverance Center, where her father, Bishop Jerome Rogers, is pastor.

Author
Nikita Ford

My name is Nikita Ford, I was born and raised in Beloit, WI. I am a mother of 5 and grandmother of 5.

Rubies with a Purpose is my first book and I'm so excited so share my testimony and encourage other women. Being a survivor of domestic violence I wanted to write a book that reminds women that we are precious jewels and we all have a purpose in life no matter what we have been through.

Nikita Ford
 Founder of Rubies with a Purpose
(502) 516-6937
rubieswithapurpose@gmail.com

Reverend _Jessie M._ Butler, M.Div

Reverend Jessie M. Butler was licensed by Triumph Baptist Church on November 24, 2002, and upon recommendation of the called council of churches of The Pennsylvania Eastern Keystone Baptist Association, under the pastorate of the Reverend Dr. James S. Hall Jr., Triumph Baptist Church, Philadelphia, Pennsylvania, she was ordained on July 10, 2005.

Reverend Butler, a religious educator taught at Mercer Christian Academy, and found her niche in Christian Education at Triumph Baptist Church. She preached, taught Bible study, developed a Church Leadership Training curriculum, and oversaw numerous ministries under the Christian Education umbrella.

In her foresight to be a dedicated minister helping others, she served as pulpit supply in numerous states and participated in various conferences through preaching, leadership training, workshops, and lecturers. Her voice empowers others to live through compassionate words and encourages the hearers to keep moving forward in their faith.

She is the Founding Pastor of Power to Live Community Church of Pemberton, N.J. When she preaches, teaches, and counsels, the congregation often hears her say: Faith is your victory. God loves you. You are important to Him. Nothing is impossible for God. God is the answer.

She has sought to educate herself through the years. She graduated from Mercer County School of Nursing in 1972. Reverend Butler is a 2000 Cum Laude graduate of Cairn University in Langhorne, Pennsylvania, with a Bachelor of Science in Bible and History, and is a 2004 honor graduate from Princeton Theological Seminary, Princeton, New Jersey, where she earned her Master of Divinity. As a lifelong learner, she will continue to pursue her goal of a Doctorate in Leadership.

Rev. Jessie M. Butler (Cont.)

She is a contributing author in Voices of the 21st Century (Hope of Vision Publishing, 2013) and the author of Row in the Storm (Hope of Vision Publishing, 2018).

Reverend Butler is the devoted wife of Deacon Frank Butler Jr., a business major and graduate of the College of New Jersey, computer operator and union master plumber. He is the owner of Butler Plumbing and Heating. They raised three children, Kimberly, Anthony, and Chinua, have seven grandchildren, and eleven great-grandchildren.

Reverend Butler looks forward to each day spent serving, for the expansion of God's kingdom, marked by faith, integrity, scholarship, compassion, and joy.

Her favorite scripture is Proverbs 18:10. "The name of the Lord is a strong tower; the righteous run to it and are safe." (NKJ)

E-Mail: jessiebutlerministry@gmail.com

Church Phone: (609) 894-0002

Author: Lena M. Lee

Lena Marie Lee, a native of southeastern Pennsylvania who is a multi-talented, published Author, Artist and Inventor is also CEO/Founder of LM Wizard, LLC, a small technology design corporation. However, her love for art and fashion design started at a very early age. Lena comes from a long line of artists, designers, musicians and inventors. She enjoys drawing, designing, inventing, reading and writing, and took a natural gift for drawing and sketching and incorporated that love throughout her life. While in high school, Lee was part of the fashion design ads for shows held at the school. She also drew portraits for friends and classmates. In 2000, Lee was awarded a Utility Patent for dolls she invented that are of no race or nationality called "The Lollipop Tots" and has written 16 copyrighted, short stories regarding the dolls. Her first book, entitled, "The Lollipop Tots – The Great Parade" which was published 2024. The story teaches children about friendship and manners. She is also the author of "Panic in the Jungle", a suspense thriller available on Amazon, was published in 2021. Her latest book, part of a 6 book series, "After the Sun Rises," is presently available only on kindle. However, the hardcover will be published sometime later in 2024.

Author Lena Lee

The story teaches
children about friendship and manners. She is also the author of "Panic in the
Jungle", a suspense thriller available on Amazon, which was published in 2021. Her latest
book, part of a six-book series entitled "After the Sun Rises," is presently available only on
Kindle. however, the hardcover will be published sometime later in 2024.
Along with her first patent, Lee also has a second "patent pending" status
for a multi-functional laptop called the Wizard that can manually copy and print
documents which she won first place award for most creative innovative idea in
2014 from West Chester University. Her luxury maxi dress line, the
"Kaleidoscope" collection is an extension of her creative gift. Along with her dress
collection, which was sold through Thunderlily Boutique in New York, Lena has
embarked on the making of her signature perfume, "Reign", the fragrance fit for a
Queen. Inspired from one of her dresses from the Kaleidoscope collection, Lee
continues to design for women who embrace beauty and fashion. She has
received an honorary book award from BookFest for "Panic in the Jungle" and was
included in Stanford Who & #39's , Who and Marquis, Who & 39' s Who. Lee credits much of
her gift of creativity to her Lord and Savior and her late father, Jay Henry Lee, who
also was a highly influential artist, engineer and inventor.

AUTHOR DEBORAH MORRISON

Deborah Morrison is the Founder and CEO of Heal Leah Ministries, Inc. (a women's ministry centered on hope and restoration, cultivating healing, and unleashing their God-given purpose, by embracing the journey to wholeness). She brings over 18 years of diverse experience in ministry leadership. Actively engaged in her community, Deborah spearheads various outreach initiatives. In addition to her ministerial roles, she hosts a weekly Facebook Live broadcast Motivational Moments with Pastor Deborah.

Pastor Deborah embodies the roles of a dedicated student, teacher, and preacher of God's Word, witnessing lives transformed, minds renewed, and evident deliverance. She identifies herself as a "Repairer of the Breach," carrying a God-given burden to witness women experience the same freedom and deliverance she has personally encountered. She finds deep fulfillment in acknowledging that God transforms our initial brokenness, meant to cause harm, into a source of healing for others. Pastor Deborah frequently says, "Healing is a journey, not a destination," emphasizing the ongoing and transformative nature of the healing process. For more information, visit www.healleahminstries.com

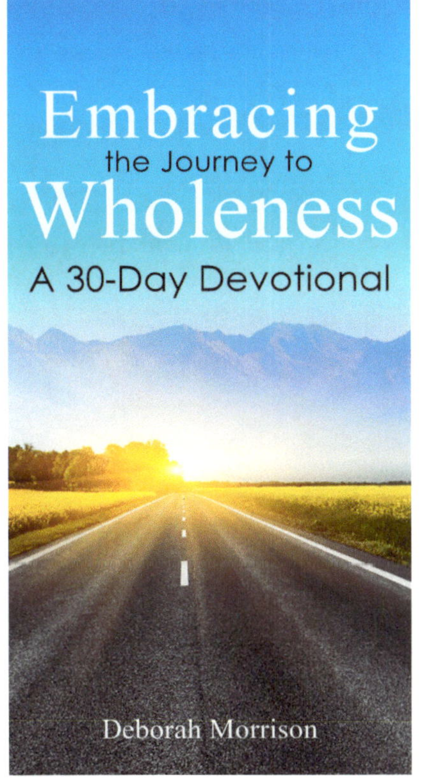

THANKS TO GOD FOR THIS VISION!

With heartfelt gratitude, I lift my voice in thanks to God for his divine vision that has brought such extraordinary authors and poets to my midst. Their brilliance and creativity have enriched my life and the lives of countless others. I am humbled by the gift of their presence and the beauty they bring to the literary world.

I give thanks to God for orchestrating the perfect alignment of circumstances that allowed me to connect with these wonderful souls.

It is a true testament to His divine plan and the power of his guiding hand. I am in awe of the ways in which God has brought us together, weaving a tapestry of talent, wisdom, and inspiration that continues to inspire us all.

In this moment of gratitude, I acknowledge God's grace and providence for granting me the opportunity to collaborate and learn from these gifted authors and poets.

May we continue to be guided by God's wisdom and love as we journey together, united by our shared passion for literature, the written and spoken word.

Paulette R. Henson

In This Issue...

*For information on anything BWA
please email us -
we'd love to hear from you!*

BWA Team

P. Henson	CEO, Founder
Denise L.	Design
Felicia K.	Administrative
Khoury S.	Technical
Michelle H.	Education
Taryn L.	Operations
Valerie S.	Editing
Taniesha C-P	Contributor

author.submissions@blackwomenauthors.net

DIVA

BLACK WOMEN AUTHORS
PAULETTE HENSON